Henry Hiliard] [Earl

Fall River

And its Manufactories

Henry Hiliard] [Earl

Fall River
And its Manufactories

ISBN/EAN: 9783337235901

Printed in Europe, USA, Canada, Australia, Japan

Cover: Foto ©Suzi / pixelio.de

More available books at **www.hansebooks.com**

FALL RIVER:

AND ITS

MANUFACTORIES.

1803—1878.

With Valuable Statistical Tables,

From Official Sources.

Fifth Edition.   Revised and Enlarged.

FALL RIVER, MASS.
BENJAMIN EARL & SON.
1878.

Almy, Milne & Co., Printers. Fall River, Mass.

CONTENTS.

	Page
FALL RIVER.—Location, Water Power, and Growth in Cotton Manufacture,	5
CHRONOLOGICAL TABLE OF EVENTS,	10
BANKS AND SAVINGS INSTITUTIONS,	21
INDIAN NAMES OF FALL RIVER AND VICINITY,	22
POPULATION TABLES.—1810–1877,	24
NO. OF NAMES ON VOTERS LISTS AND VOTES CAST IN 1877.	24
VALUATION TABLES.—1854-1877,	25
COTTON SPINNING IN THE U. S.,	26
WEEKLY PRODUCTION OF PRINT CLOTH MILLS IN FALL RIVER,	27
FALL RIVER PRINT CLOTH MARKET.— Sept., 1876, to Sept., 1877,	28
PRINT WORKS IN THE UNITED STATES.— Capacity, Production, &c ,	30
STATISTICS OF COTTON MANUFACTORIES.— Capital, Spindles, Looms, &c.,	32
STATISTICS OF COTTON MANUFACTORIES.— Location, Cotton Used, Production, &c.,	34
PAY-DAYS OF THE CORPORATIONS.	36
ORGANIZATION OF CORPORATIONS.—With Date of Annual Meeting,	37

Fall River, Mass:
Its Location, Water Power, and Growth in Cotton Manufacture.

———— ➤ ————

FALL RIVER is a City and port of entry
of Bristol County, Massachusetts, and is
pleasantly situated on a rather abrupt el-
evation of land, rising at the head of Mt. Hope
Bay, an arm of Narragansett Bay. It comprises
an area of about thirty-six and a half square
miles, and about 23,330 acres including both
land and water. It is eminently a manufacturing place, but is specially noted for its Cotton
Manufactories; while its favorable position as
regards railway and steamboat communications,
its improvements in commercial and mechani-
cal industry, and its recent almost unparalled
increase in population and wealth have given it
a name and importance second to none in the
Commonwealth.

In the union of hydraulic power and navigable waters, it is perhaps without a parallel upon the American Continent. Its hydraulic power is derived from a small stream — Fall River — whence the name of the city, which has its source, or is in reality the outflow of a chain of ponds lying two miles east of the Bay, covering an area of 3,500 acres, and having a length of about eight miles, and an average breadth of three quarters of a mile. They are mostly supplied by perennial springs, though receiving the outlets of several other sheets of water. The extent of country drained, is comparatively small,— the whole water-shed being not over 20,000 acres, and the quantity of power therefore is to be attributed to the springs alluded to, and to the great and rapid fall of the river, which in less than half a mile is more than 129 feet. The flow of the river is one hundred and twenty-one and a half cubic feet per second, or 9,841,500,000 Imperial gallons in a year of three hundred days of ten hours each.

The remarkable advantages of this river as a mill stream have been increased by building a dam at the outlet of the ponds, which gives the water an additional fall of two feet; and its lower banks are entirely built up with large man-

ufacturing establishments, which so rapidly suc-
ceed each other, as scarcely to leave space between some of the buildings, sufficient for light
and air. The river for almost its entire length
runs upon a granite bed, and for much of the
distance is confined between high banks, also
of granite. Differing therefore from most other
water-powers, this one allows the entire space
between its banks to be occupied, and most of
the water wheels connected with the older factories are placed directly in the bed of the river. Moreover, while the river affords an almost
uniform and constant supply of water, it is never subject to excess, and an injury in conse-
quence of a freshet has never yet been known.
The river is perfectly controllable, and thus it
is that the mills were built directly across the
river, the wheels placed in the bed of the river,
and yet from an excess of water, no damage was
to be apprehended. In later years, however,
most of the breast wheels employed in these
older mills, have been supplanted by the mod-
ern appliances of turbine wheels and steam
power.

With the increase of wealth and skill in manufacture, and the entrance upon the stage of ac-
tion of younger men of enterprise and ambition,

new projects were formed, and as the older mills
occupied all available space upon the river
banks, new situations were sought out and ap-
propriated, and the "New Mills" so called,
were first erected on the margin of the ponds
to the south and east of the city, and of which
the stream is the outlet, and afterwards in the
northerly and southerly sections of the city, on
the banks of the Taunton river and Laurel lake.

The number of incorporated companies for
the manufacture of cotton goods is now thirty-
three, owning forty mills, or forty-three, count-
ing those having two mills under one roof, with
an incorporated capital of $14,565,000 but a
probable investment of $30,000,000, containing
1.284,701 spindles, and 30,577 looms.

The latest statistics, report the total number
of mills in the United States as 847, containing
186,975 looms and 9,415,383 spindles, manufacturing 588,000,000 yards of print cloths per an-
num. Of these, New England has 489 mills,
containing 148,189 looms and 7,538,369 spindles,
manufacturing 481,000,000 yards of print cloths.
Fall River has thus over 1-8th of all the spindles in the country, or 1-6th of those in New
England, and manufactures over a half of all
the print cloths.

The following table will show the number of spindles in the mills of Fall River at the close of each year respectively.

	1869,— 540,614.	
1865,—265,328.	1870.— 544,606.	1874,—1,258,508.
1866,—403,624.	1871,— 788,138.	1875,--1,269,048.
1867,—470,360.	1872,—1,094,702.	1876,- 1,274,265.
1868,—537,416.	1873,—1,212.694.	1877,—1,284,701.

Fall River is 49 miles south of Boston, 183 miles north-east of New York, 17 miles south of Taunton, 18 miles south-east of Providence, 14 miles west of New Bedford and 18 miles north of Newport. Daily lines of Steamers connect Fall River, Providence, Newport and New York, while three lines of Railways give ample passenger and freight communications inland.

Fall River was formerly a part of Freetown, and was incorporated as a separate town in 1803. Its name was soon after changed to Troy, but in 1834 its old appellation was restored. Its Indian name was "Quequeteant" signifying the "*place* of falling water," and that of the river "Quequechan" which signifies "falling water" or "quick running water," hence its appropriate name of Fall River. "Watuppa" the Indian name of the ponds on the east and by which they are still called, signifies "boats" or the "place of boats."

Fall River was incorporated a City in 1854.

Chronological Table of Important Events

In the History of Fall River.

————o————

1656.

July 3. The territory east of Taunton River, (including Fall River,) granted to certain Freemen by the General Court at Plymouth, and called the "Freemen's Purchase."

1659.

April 2. Same territory acquired from the Indians by purchase.

1675.

June 22. King Philip's War begun by an attack on Swansea. July 8. Almy's Peasfield Fight, Tiverton. July 18. Pocasset Swamp Fight, Tiverton.

1676,

Aug. 6. Weetamoe, Squaw Sachem of Pocasset, drowned near Slade's Ferry. Aug. 12, King Philip killed at Mt. Hope.   Aug. 28. Annawan, King Philip's chief captain, captured, and soon after executed at Plymouth.

1676.

Close of Indian Wars in Massachusetts.

1680.

The territory east of Mount Hope Bay, including Tiverton, acquired by deeds from the General Court at Plymouth, and from the Indians. It was called the "Pocasset Purchase," and was settled by Col. Church and the ancestors of the present Bordens and Durfees. The town was called "Pocasset." This is the FIRST SETTLEMENT of Fall River territory.

Thomas Durfee, of Portsmouth, R. I., supposed to be the ancestor of most of those who bear his name in this vicinity, bought one-sixtieth of the Pocasset Purchase for £34. This tract is probably the territory now occupied in part by the South Park.

1683.

Freetown, including the present territory of Fall River, incorporated.

1691.

Col. Church became proprietor of $26\frac{1}{2}$ shares ($26\frac{1}{2}$-30ths) of a piece of land thirty rods wide, adjacent to the stream and including the Water Power on the South side of the river, west of Main Street, and on both sides east of Main street, and extending to the Ponds. John Borden of Portsmouth, R. I., probably bought the other $3\frac{1}{2}$ shares. This strip, a reservation from the Pocasset Purchase, contained 66 acres, and was valued at about £225.

1694.

Pocasset incorporated and called Tiverton, from a town in Devonshire, England.

1684 — 1700.

Disagreement as to boundary line between Freetown and Tiverton.

1700.

Boundary line agreed upon, and all the Water Power included in Tiverton.

1702.

A small piece or strip of land, a reservation from the Freemen's Purchase, lying on the north side of the stream and west of Main Street, bought by John Borden, of Ports mouth, R. I. In 1714 Col. Church sold out his 26½ shares of the Pocasset Reservation for £1000 to the same John Borden, owner of the other 31½ shares, who thus became possessor of the whole of the Water Power and most of the land now forming the centre of the city, together with a strip east to the Watuppa Pond. This John Borden is supposed to be the ancestor of all who bear his name in this vicinity.

1703.

Col Church erected a saw mill, grist mill and Fulling Mill on the stream, south side, near the south end of Granite Block.

1740.

Dispute concerning the boundary line between the colonies of Massachusetts and Rhode Island. A Royal Commission appointed to determine the true boundary of each.

1746.

The award of the Commissioners confirmed by the King, though appealed from by both colonies. Ex-parte lines run by Rhode Island, but found incorrect when revised by Massachusetts in 1791.

1747.

Tiverton transferred from Massachusetts to Rhode Island, and the centre of the village of Fall River, together with the Water Power, transferred from Tiverton to Freetown, and thus continued under the jurisdiction of Massachusetts.

1776.

July 15. The inhabitants of Freetown declared for the Independence of the Colonies.

1778.

May 25. 150 British Troops attacked the village of Fall River. Repulsed with the loss of two men, by a company (30) of local militia, under Col. Joseph Durfee.

1803.

Fall River set off from Freetown and incorporated, — 18 Dwellings and 100 Inhabitants.

1803.

The first Town House was established at Steep Brook, the then centre of business, in 1805. In 1825, a new Town House was erected on land now occupied by the North Cemetery. In 1836, this building was removed to Town Avenue, and occupied until the completion of the new Town Hall and Market Building, erected after the "Great Fire," on Main Street. In 1845-6, the present City Hall Building, built of Fall River granite was erected in Market Square, at an expense of $65,000, including lot, foundation, side walks, furniture, &c. In 1872-3, this building was entirely remodelled (the original walls only being left) and rebuilt, with the addition of a Mansard roof, tower, clock, bell, &c., at a cost of $200,000.

1804.

Name of "Fall River" changed to "Troy," and continued so for 30 years. In 1834, changed back again to "Fall River."

1811.

Jan. 21. Post Office established; first mail received February 12.

A Cotton Mill, the first in this vicinity, erected at Globe Village by Col. Joseph Durfee and others. This building (burnt in Dec. 1838) stood on the north-east corner of South Main and Globe Sts., and was converted into a Print Works (the Globe) in 1829. Its first

1811.

goods were printed in September, 1830. The first cotton mill with machinery on the Arkwright principle, was erected in Pawtucket, R. I., by Samuel Slater, in 1790. In 1812,there were in Rhode Island, 33 Cotton Factories containing 30,663 spindles. In Massachusetts, there were 20 mills containing 17,361 spindles, Previous to 1812, the mills only spun the yarn, the weaving being done by hand looms in the neighboring farm-houses.

1813.

First Cotton Mills, Troy (stone) and F. R. Manufactory (wood), erected in Fall River; the latter commenced operations in Oct., 1813, the former in 1814. Both were organized in March, 1813.

1821.

The Fall River Iron Works Company formed. Incorporated in 1825. First established at the foot of the stream, west of the Annawan Mill. Removed to its present locality in 1840. Enlarged in 1841. Burned in May 1843, and rebuilt the same year; burned again in Feb. 1859, and immediately rebuilt.

1824.

Robeson's Print Works started in north end of Satinet Factory. Removed to present site in 1827. In 1830, organized as the Fall River Print Works. Incorporated in 1848. In 1858-64 altered into a Cotton Mill.

1825.

The manufacture of Woolen Goods commenced in the Satinet Factory, standing where the Pocasset Mill now stands. Succeeded in 1849 by the Wamsutta Steam Woollen Mill on "Mosquito Island" a promontory near the outlet of the pond.

The Fall River Bank established.

1826.

The first newspaper, the FALL RIVER MONITOR, (Weekly) established.

Horse-Boat put on at Slade's Ferry.

1827.

Steamer Hancock commenced running regularly between Fall River and Providence. Other steamers the Babcock, Experiment, Rushlight and Wadsworth, had previously attempted to establish communication between this and other places but with only partial success. The Hancock was succeeded in 1832 by steamer King Philip. The King Philip was succeeded in 1845 by the steamer Bradford Durfee. July 17, 1874, Steamer Richard Borden placed on the route.

May 19. Marco Bozzaris, a steamer, advertised to run between Dighton and New York, stopping at Fall River—"Passengers to be taken by Stage from Dighton to Boston."

1828.

First Savings Bank (Fall River) established.

1829.

Daniel Page died, last male of Pocasset tribe of Indians; active on the colonial side during the Revolutionary War.

1830.

Globe Print Works commenced running, Name changed to Bay State Print Works in 1856.

1834.

Name of the town Troy, changed back to Fall River.

American Print Works established. Enlarged in 1867, but on Dec, 15, 1867, entirely destroyed by fire, with a loss of over $1,000,000 In 1868-9, rebuilt and greatly enlarged.

1835.

The first Incorporated Library (Athenæum) opened

1838.

First Thread Mill (O. Chace's) built.

1840.

Main Street set with two rows of Elms.

1843.

July 2. The "Great Fire," burning over 20 acres of the very centre of the village. Over 200 buildings burned. Loss upwards of $500,000.

1844.

Question of boundry line between Massachusetts and Rhode Island again agitated. In 1852, the subject referred to the Courts. In 1862, the present boundary line established by the United States Courts.

1845.

June. Fall River Railroad opened to Myricks.

1846.

Dec. Fall River Railroad opened to South Braintree, connecting there with the Old Colony Railroad. In 1854, Old Colony and Fall River Railroads united.

1847.

Steamboat line to New York established by the Bay State Steamboat Company, with the steamers Bay State and Empire State.
Fall River Gas Works built.

1850.

Fall River High School established.

1852.

American Linen Company incorporated and first Mill built. This was the first enterprise of the kind in the country, and a success in its manufacturing department; but as cotton and thin woolen fabrics were soon after generally substituted for linen goods, in 1858 the machinery was mostly changed to that for the manufacture of Print Cloths.

1854.

April 12. Fall River incorporated a City.
April 23. The Charter accepted by vote of the citizens.

1860.

Free Public Library established by the City.

1861.

April 12. Commencement of the Civil War in America. June 11. First troops from Fall River, (Cos. A and B, 7th Regt.) mustered into the U. S. Service. From 1861 to May 26, 1865, the close of the war, Fall River furnished 1,770 men, viz: 1.273 Army, 497 Navy.

1863.

Nov. 19. First passenger train to Stone Bridge.

1865.

May 22. First Passenger train on Fall River and Warren Railroad.

1869.

Dec. 25. Fire Alarm Telegraph established.

1873.

Aug. 1. Free Mail Delivery (8 carriers) established.
Dec. 26. Dedication of new City Hall, after two years spent in remodeling and rebuilding.

1874.

Jan. 8. Water from Watuppa Pond first introduced into the City. The laying of Water

1874.

Pipes begun in May, 1872. Engine House for supply commenced in June, 1872.

Sept. 19. Granite Mill Fire, resulting in loss of 23 killed and 33 Wounded.

1875.

Jan. 10. Mt. Hope Bay frozen over. Navigation suspended on the 20th, and not resumed till Feb. 25th. Feb. 22. Many people and loaded teams passed on ice from Steamboat Wharf to Providence Ferry.

March 10. First clear passage to Bristol Ferry — large ice floes still in the bay.

Nov. 10. O. C. R. R. Bridge at Slade's Ferry, completed. Opened to public travel, Jan. 4, 1876. Work begun on the Piers Oct. 8, 1874. Tested Nov. 9, 1875. Accepted Nov. 10, 1875. The Bridge is of iron and cost $300,000.

Dec. 6. First passenger train to Providence via New Bridge at Slade's Ferry.

Dec. 13. Dedication of new Central Congregational Church.

Dec. 16. First passenger train via Fall River Railroad to New Bedford.

1876.

Jan. 6. Dedication of the Academy of Music.

June 29. American Linen Co.'s Mill No, 2. burned.

1877.

June 26. Dedication of New Court Rooms for the Superior Court in Borden Block

Nov. 17. Border City Mill No. 1, totally destroyed by fire.

Banks of the City of Fall River, Mass., from the Official Reports, Oct., 1877.

Name	Estab.	President.	Cashier.	Capital.	Surplus & Int.	Disc't Day.
Fall River Nat'l Bank,	1825	G. H. Hathaway,	F. H. Gifford,	400,000	143,449	Mon.
National Union Bank,	1830	Cook Borden,	D. A. Chapin,	300,000	59,241	Fri.
Massasoit Nat'l Bank,	1846	Chas. P. Stickney,	L. Borden,	200,000	168,520	Wed.
Metacomet Nat'l Bank,	1853	Jefferson Borden,	A. S. Tripp,	600,000	323,072	Mon. / Thu.
Pocasset Nat'l Bank,	1854	Weaver Osborn,	E. E. Hathaway	200,000	98,570	Tues.
Second National Bank,	1857	S. Angier Chace,	C. J. Holmes,	150,000	58,503	Thrs.
First National Bank,	1864	John S. Brayton,	H. A. Brayton,	400,000	386,466	Daily.
				2,250,000	1,237,821	

Savings Banks of Fall River, Mass., from the Official Reports, Oct., 1877.

Name.	Incor.	Treasurer.	Deposits.	Depos'rs.	Disc't Day.	Dividends.
Fall River Savings Bank,	1828	C. A. Bassett,	6,039,197.87	11,760	Tues.	Apr. Oct.
Citizens' Savings Bank,	1851	E. E. Hathaway,	1,871,974.50	2,767	Fri.	June. Dec.
Five Cent Savings Bank,	1856	C. J. Holmes,	1,443,934.68	5,489	Mon.	June. Dec.
Union Savings Bank,	1869	D. A. Chapin,	671,384.56	1,384	Fri.	Nov. May.
			10,026,491.61	21,400		

Indian Names of Fall River and Vicinity.

ANNAWAN-1600(?)-1676. "An officer." A Wampanoag, one of King Philip's most famous Captains.

CANONICUS—1557-(!)-1647. Chief of the Narragansetts; a friend of Roger Williams.

CORBITANT—1530-(?)-1624. Sachem of Pocasset Tribe; chief residence at Gardner's Neck, Swansea.

KING PHILIP—1628-(?)-1676. English name of Metacomet. youngest son of Massasoit, and his successor, in 1662, as Chief of the Wampanoags.

MASSASOIT—1581-1661. Sachem of the Wampanoags and Chief of the Indian Confederacy formed of tribes in Eastern Massachusetts and Rhode Island. A staunch friend of the English.

METACOMET—Indian name of King Philip, second son of Massasoit.

MONTAUP—"The Head." Indian name of Mount Hope.

NARRAGANSETT—"At the Point." Indian tribe on west side of Narragansett Bay.

NIANTIC—"At the River Point." Sub-tribe of the Narragansetts.

POCASSET—"At the opening of the Strait," I. e., Bristol Ferry into Mount Hope Bay. Indian name of territory, now including Fall River and Tiverton.

QUEQUETEANT—"The PLACE of falling water." Indian name of Fall River.

QUEQUECHAN—"It leaps or bounds." Indian name of the stream—Fall River—signifying falling water or quick running water.

SAGAMORE—"A leader." Title of Indian Chief.

TECUMSEH—1770-1813. Chief of the Shawnees : distinguished for his eloquence, bravery and manly virtues. Prominent on the Western frontier in the war of 1812.

WAMPANOAG—"East landers," i. e., east of Narragansett Bay. Indian tribe dwelling north and east of Narragansett Bay, west of Mount Hope Bay.

WAMSUTTA—1625-(?)-1662. English name, Alexander. Eldest son and successor of Massasoit in 1661.

WATUPPA—"Boats or the place of boats." Name of Ponds east of the city.

WEETAMOE—1620-(?)-1676. "Wise, shrewd, cunning." Daughter and successor of Corbitant as Sachem of the Pocasset tribe; residence at Fall River; drowned while crossing Slade's Ferry.

STATISTICAL

—AND—

REFERENCE TABLES.

JANUARY, 1878.

POPULATION — 1810-1877.

POPULATION OF FALL RIVER AT VARIOUS TIMES.

1810	1,296	1859	12,524
1820	1,594	1860	13,240
1830	4,159	1861	14,026
1840	6,738	1862*	17,461
1844	9,054	1863	15,495
1845	10,290	1864	17,114
1846	11,174	1865	17,525
1847	11,646	1866	19,262
1848	10,922	1867	21,174
1849	11,003	1868	23,023
1850	11,170	1869	25,099
1851	10,786	1870	27,191
1852	11,605	1871	28,291
1853	12,285	1872	34,835
1854	12,700	1873	38,464
1855	12,680	1874	43,289
1856	12,926	1875	45,160
1857	12,395	1876	44,356
1858	12,815	1877	45,113

*The increase in population in 1862 was owing to the annexation of the Town of Fall River. R. I., which contained a population of about 3,590.

NO. OF NAMES ON VOTERS' LISTS CORRECTED TO DEC. 1, 1877.

Wards,	1	2	3	4	5	6	Total.
City Election,	848	855	903	1108	936	835	5.485
State Election,	711	698	735	911	845	711	4.611

OFFICIAL RETURN OF VOTES.

Wards,	1	2	3	4	5	6	Total.
Republican,	366	237	396	421	668	544	2,632
Democratic,	390	588	449	598	162	169	2.356

VALUATION, &c., 1854-1877.

VALUATION, TAX, &C., FOR THE LAST 24 YEARS.

Year.	Valuation.	Tax.	Amt. Raised by Taxation.	No. Polls.
1854,	8,939,215	$5.80	$56,523.70	3,117
1855,	9,768,420	5.60	59,425.15	3,148
1856,	9,888,070	6.20	66,078.26	3,181
1857,	10,041,610	7.40	83,161.61	3,241
1858,	9,923,495	7.20	77,929.35	3,208
1859,	10,700,250	7.00	79,583.25	3,121
1860,	11,522,650	7.40	90,124.61	3,238
1861,	11,261,065	8.60	102,162.04	3,544
1862,	12,497,720	11.00	146,045.30	4,288
1863,	12,696,105	11.50	154,218.76	4,105
1864,	11,057,645	18.00	207,731.61	4,304
1865,	12,134,990	16.50	209,272.20	4,461
1866,	12,762,534	17.50	232,827.62	4,740
1867,	15,220,628	17.00	269,020.95	5,135
1868,	17,919,192	14.00	262,872.74	6,002
1869,	21,398,525	15.60	346,310.99	6,247
1870,	23,612,214	15.30	374,753.22	6,743
1871,	29,141,117	13.00	392,974.15	7,070
1872,	37,841,294	12.00	471,835.53	8,870
1873,	47,410,246	13.00	636,451.61	10,020
1874,	49,995,110	12.80	662,486.11	11,119
1875,	51,401,467	14.50	768,464.37	11,571
1876,	48,920,485	15.20	764,629.41	10,519
1877,	47,218,320	15 50	753,735.96	10,926

In 1840, the number of taxable polls was 1,603. The valuation of real estate was $1,678,603; of personal estate, $1,310,865; total, $2,989,468.

COTTON SPINNING IN THE UNITED STATES.

Comparative Statement of the Number and Capacity of Cotton Mills, and Print Cloths Manufactured in the United States.

	No. of Mills.	No. of Spindles.	No. of Looms.
United States	817	9,415,383	186,975
New England	498	7,538,369	148,189
Fall River	43	1,284,701	30,577

	U. S.	N. E.	F. R.
Print Cloths M'f'd,	588,000,000	481,000,000	363,000,000

No. of Spindles in Fall River.

1865	265,328	1871	780,183
1866	403,624	1872	1,094,702
1867	470,360	1873	1,212,694
1868	537,416	1874	1,258,508
1869	540,614	1875	1,269,048
1870	544,606	1876	1,274,265
		1877	1,284,701.

WEEKLY PRODUCTION
OF PRINT CLOTH MILLS IN FALL RIVER.

Corporation.	No. of Mills.	Weekly Production. in Pieces.
American Linen Co.	2	10,000 Pieces.
Annawan Manufactory.	1	1,000
Barnard Manufacturing Co.	1	4,000
Border City Mills..	2	10,000
Chace Mills.	1	7,500
*Crescent Mills.	1	1,000
*Davol Mills.	2	1,000
Durfee Mills.	2	10,000
Fall River Manufactory.	1	3,000
Fall River Print Works.	1	1,500
Flint Mills.	1	5,500
Granite Mills.	2	10,000
Mechanics' Mills.	1	7,000
Merchants' Manufacturing Co	2	10,000
Metacomet Mill.	1	3,000
Narragansett Mills.	1	4,000
Osborn Mills.	1	5,000
*Pocasset Manufacturing Co.	2	2,000
R. Borden Manufacturing C .	1	5,500
Robeson Mills.	1	3,000
Sagamore Mills.	1	5,000
Shove Mills.	1	5,500
Slade Mills.	1	4,500
Stafford Mills.	1	4,500
Tecumseh Mills.	2	5,500
Troy C. & W., Manufactory.	2	4,500
Union Mill Co.	2	5,000
Wampanoag Mills.	1	3,500
Weetamoe Mills.	1	4,500
		146,500

*Wide Cloth Mills.

FALL RIVER PRINT CLOTH MARKET,

For the Year Ending Sept. 1, 1877.

Week Ending		Stock on Hand.	Sales of Week.	Price per Yard.	Price Md'lg Cott'n in N. York.
1876		Pieces.			
Sept.	2	70,000	115,000	$4\frac{1}{2}$	$11\frac{7}{8}$
	9	115,000	None.	$4\frac{3}{8}$	$11\frac{5}{8}$
	16	85,000	450,000	$4\frac{1}{2}$	$11\frac{3}{8}$
	23	60,000	390,000	$4\frac{7}{8}$	$11\frac{1}{4}$
	30	80,000	83,500	$4\frac{7}{8}$	11
Oct.	7	95,000	46,000	5	$10\frac{7}{8}$
	14	130,000	None.	$4\frac{7}{8}$	$10\frac{7}{8}$
	21	140,000	10,000	$4\frac{3}{4}$	$10\frac{7}{8}$
	28	160,000	None.	$4\frac{1}{4}$	11
Nov.	4	190,000	13,000	$4\frac{1}{4}$	$11\frac{5}{8}$
	11	150,000	343,500	$4\frac{1}{2}$	$12\frac{1}{8}$
	18	165,000	212,000	$4\frac{1}{2}$	12
	25	190,000	5,000	$4\frac{3}{8}$	$12\frac{1}{8}$
Dec.	2	150,000	186,000	$4\frac{1}{2}$	$12\frac{1}{4}$
	9	140,000	48,000	$4\frac{5}{8}$	$12\frac{1}{8}$
	16	125,000	100,000	4 9–16	$12\frac{1}{4}$
	23	71,000	338,000	4 11–16	$12\frac{1}{4}$
	30	25,000	125,000	$4\frac{3}{4}$	$12\frac{1}{2}$
1877					
Jan.	6	25,000	178,000	$4\frac{3}{4}$	$13\frac{1}{4}$
	13	75,000	20,000	$4\frac{7}{8}$	$13\frac{1}{8}$
	20	83,000	201,000	$4\frac{7}{8}$	$13\frac{1}{8}$
	27	50,000	207,000	5	$13\frac{1}{4}$
Feb.	3	40,000	219,000	$5\frac{1}{4}$	$12\frac{7}{8}$
	10	39,000	448,000	5 5–16	$12\frac{7}{8}$
	17	34,000	67,000	$5\frac{1}{4}$	$12\frac{7}{8}$
	24	60,000	13,000	$4\frac{7}{8}$	$12\frac{1}{2}$
Mar.	3	28,000	50,000	$4\frac{7}{8}$	$12\frac{1}{2}$

FALL RIVER PRINT CLOTH MARKET,

For the Year Ending Sept. 1, 1877.

Week Ending	Stock on Hand.	Sales of Week.	Price per Yard.	Price Md'lg Cott'n in N. York.
1877	Pieces.			
Mar. 10	25,000	35,000	$4\frac{3}{4}$	$12\frac{1}{4}$
17	65,000	5,000	$4\frac{1}{2}$	$11\frac{5}{8}$
24	80,000	8,000	$4\frac{1}{4}$	$11\frac{1}{2}$
31	120,000	None.	4	$11\frac{5}{8}$
April 7	200,000	20,000	4	$11\frac{1}{2}$
14	200,000	15,000	4 1-16	$11\frac{3}{8}$
21	330,000	276,000	4 1-16	$11\frac{1}{4}$
28	390,000	50,000	4	11
May 5	432,000	75,000	4	$11\frac{1}{4}$
12	450,000	79,000	$4\frac{1}{8}$	$10\frac{7}{8}$
19	350,000	356,000	$4\frac{1}{4}$	$10\frac{7}{8}$
26	365,000	166,000	$4\frac{1}{4}$	$11\frac{3}{8}$
June 2	331,000	333,000	$4\frac{3}{8}$	$11\frac{3}{8}$
9	353,000	95,000	$4\frac{3}{8}$	$11\frac{5}{8}$
16	360,000	65,000	$4\frac{3}{8}$	$11\frac{3}{4}$
23	354,000	175,000	$4\frac{3}{8}$	$11\frac{3}{4}$
30	380,000	50,000	$4\frac{3}{8}$	$12\frac{1}{4}$
July 7	455,000	69,000	$4\frac{3}{8}$	$12\frac{1}{4}$
14	554,000	None.	$4\frac{3}{8}$	$12\frac{1}{4}$
21	635,000	None.	$4\frac{1}{4}$	$12\frac{1}{4}$
28	725,000	5,000	$4\frac{3}{8}$	$12\frac{1}{4}$
Aug. 4	790,000	23,000	$4\frac{1}{4}$	$11\frac{7}{8}$
11	875,000	10,000	$4\frac{1}{8}$	$11\frac{1}{2}$
18	960,000	15,000	$4\frac{1}{4}$	$11\frac{1}{2}$
25	1,020,000	15,000	$4\frac{1}{8}$	11
Sept. 1	989,000	116,000	$3\frac{7}{8}$	11

Cotton Crop 1876-7...........4,474,069 Bales.

PRINT WORKS IN THE UNITED STATES.

Name of Print Works.	Location.
Albion,	Conshohocken, Penn.,
Allen,	Providence, R. I.,
American,	Fall River, Mass.,
Ancona,	Gloucester, N. J.,
Arnold.	North Adams, Mass.,
Ashland,	Ashland, Mass.,
Bristol,	E. Greenwich, R. I.,
Cocheco,	Dover, N. H.,
Conestoga,	Conestoga, Penn.,
Dunnell,	Pawtucket, R. I.,
Freeman,	North Adams, Mass.,
Garner & Co.,	Haverstraw and Wappinger Falls, N. Y.
Gloucester,	Gloucester, Mass.,
Hamilton,	Lawrence, Mass.,
Hartell.	Holmesburg J'nct'n, N.J.
Knickerbocker,	Southbridge, Mass.,
Mallory,	Patterson, N. J.,
Manchester,	Manchester, N. H.,
Merrimack,	Lowell, Mass.,
Oriental,	Apponaug, R. I.,
Pacific,	Lawrence, Mass.,
Passaic,	Passaic, N. J.,
Richmond,	Providence, R. I.,
Simpson,	Chester, Penn.,
Sprague's	Cranston, R. I.,
Southbridge,	Southbridge, Mass.,
Union,	Bustleton, Penn.,
Washington,	River Point, R. I.,

PRINT WORKS IN THE UNITED STATES.

Capital of Incorporated Companies.	No. of Print'g Machines.	No. Pieces of Calico Pri't'd per Week.	No. Pieces of Print Cloths made per week by the Com'y.
$300,000	4	6,000	None.
Not Incor.	11	22,000	6,300
1,000,000	21	33,000	None.
500,000	8	15,000	None.
150,000	8	14,000	7,500
Not Incor.	4	5,000	None.
"	7	12,000	2,000
1,500,000	13	20,000	7,500
Not Incor.	8	14,000	None.
700,000	12	16,000	None.
Not Incor.	7	13,000	2,000
"	42	70,000	40,000
650,000	12	18,000	5,000
1,200,000	8	15,000	5,000
Not Incor.	5	7,000	None.
600,000	6	9,000	None.
Not Incor.	4	6,000	None.
2,000,000	14	22,000	7,000
2,500,000	14	24,000	19,000
Not Incor.	10	18,000	None.
2,500,000	22	15,000	15,000
Not Incor.	7	12,000	None.
"	7	10,000	7,000
1,000,000	16	25,000	None.
Not Incor.	30	50,000	27,000
"	5	8,000	None.
"	4	6,000	None.
"	7	12,000	None.
	316	407,000	150,300

STATISTICS OF COTTON MANUFACTORIES

IN FALL RIVER.

	Corporations.	Treasurer.
1	American Linen Co.,	Walter Paine, 3d,
2	Annawan Manufactory,	Thomas S. Borden,
3	Barnard Manufg. Co.,	Nathaniel B. Borden,
4	Border City Mills,	Geo. T. Hathaway,
5	Chace Mills,	Joseph A. Baker,
6	Crescent Mills,	Alphonso S. Covel,
7	Davol Mills,	Wm. C. Davol, Jr.,
8	Durfee Mills,	David A. Brayton,
9	Fall River Manufactory,	S. Angier Chace,
10	Fall River Merino Co.,	Seth H. Wetherbee,
11	Fall River Print Works,	Andrew Robeson,
12	Flint Mills,	George H. Eddy,
13	Granite Mills,	Charles M. Shove,
14	King Philip Mills,	Elijah C. Kilburn,
15	Mechanics' Mills,	Geo. B. Durfee,
16	Merchants' Manufg. Co.,	Wm. H. Jennings,
17	Metacomet Mill,	Thos. S. Borden, Agt.,
18	Montaup Mills,	Isaac Borden,
19	Mount Hope Mill,	Jeff. Borden, Jr., Agt.,
20	Narragansett Mills,	James Waring,
21	Osborn Mills,	Joseph Healy,
22	Pocasset Manufg. Co.,	Henry S. Howe, Agt,
23	Richard Borden Mfg. Co.,	Richard B. Borden,
24	Robeson Mills,	Louis Robeson,
25	Sagamore Mills,	Geo. T. Hathaway,
26	Shove Mills,	George A. Chace,
27	Slade Mills,	Henry S. Fenner,
28	Stafford Mills,	F. H. Stafford, Agt,
29	Tecumseh Mills,	Simeon B. Chase.
30	Troy C. & W. Manuf'y,	Richard B. Borden,
31	Union Mill Co.,	S. Angier Chace,
32	Wampanoag Mills,	Walter C. Durfee,
33	Weetamoe Mills,	William Lindsey,

STATISTICS OF COTTON MANUFACTORIES
IN FALL RIVER.

	Capital.	Spindl's	Looms.	Style of Goods.
1	$400,000	82,800	1,942	Print Cloths.
2	160,000	10,016	192	" "
3	330,000	29,440	768	" "
4	1,000,000	77,878	1,884	" "
5	500,000	43,480	1,080	" "
6	500,000	33,280	744	Yd. wide fine goods.
7	- 270,000	30,496	768	Sheetings, Silesias & Fancy Cottons.
8	500,000	86,200	2,064	Print Cloths.
9	150,000	25,992	600	" "
10	90,000	1,560	15	Merino Und'wear.
11	200,000	13,600	306	Print Cloths.
12	600,000	45,712	1,065	" "
13	400,000	78,520	1,868	" "
14	500,000	39,360	824	Fine G'ds & Jac'n't.
15	750,000	53,712	1,300	Print Cloths.
16	800,000	86,820	2,000	" "
17	300,000	23,840	591	" "
18	250,000	7,200	112	Duck and Yarns.
19	200,000	9,024	216	Shirtings.
20	400,000	29,360	724	Print Cloths.
21	500,000	37,744	964	" "
22	800,000	31,584	690	P. C. Sh'gs&Shirt'gs
23	800,000	44,765	1,056	Print Cloths.
24	260,000	22,976	576	" "
25	250,000	39,566	942	" "
26	550,000	39,040	960	" "
27	550,000	37,040	875	" "
28	550,000	34,928	860	" "
29	500,000	43,056	1,052	" "
30	300,000	38,928	932	" "
31	155,000	44,784	1,050	" "
32	500,000	27,920	705	" "
33	550,000	34,080	852	" "
	$14,565,000	1,284,701	30,577	

STATISTICS OF COTTON MANUFACTORIES

IN FALL RIVER.

	Corporations.	No. Mills.	Location.
1	American Linen Co.,	2	Ferry Street,
2	Annawan Manufactory,	1	Annawan Street,
3	Barnard Mfg. Co.,	1	Quequechan St.,
4	Border City Mills,	2	North Main Road
5	Chace Mills,	1	Rodman Street,
6	Crescent Mills,	1	Eight Rod Way,
7	Davol Mills,	2	Hartwell Street,
8	Durfee Mills,	2	Pleasant Street,
9	Fall River Manufactory,	1	Pocasset Street,
10	Fall River Merino Co.,	1	Alden Street,
11	Fall River Print Works,	1	Pocasset Street,
12	Flint Mills,	1	Alden Street,
13	Granite Mills,	2	Twelfth Street,
14	King Philip Mills,	1	Laurel Lake,
15	Mechanics' Mills,	1	Mechanicsville,
16	Merchants' Mfg. Co.,	2	Fourteenth St.,
17	Metacomet Mill,	1	Annawan Street,
18	Montaup Mills,	1	Laurel Lake,
19	Mount Hope Mill,	1	Bay Street,
20	Narragansett Mills,	1	North Main Road
21	Osborn Mills,	1	Laurel Lake,
22	Pocasset Mfg. Co.,	2	Pocasset Street,
23	Richard Borden Mfg. Co.,	1	Rodman Street,
24	Robeson Mills,	1	Hartwell Street,
25	Sagamore Mills,	1	North Main Road
26	Shove Mills,	1	Laurel Lake,
27	Slade Mills,	1	Laurel Lake,
28	Stafford Mills,	1	Quarry Street,
29	Tecumseh Mills,	2	Hartwell Street,
30	Troy C. & W. Manuf'y,	2	Troy Street,
31	Union Mill Co.,	2	Pleasant Street,
32	Wampanoag Mills,	1	Quequechan St.,
33	Weetamoe Mills,	1	Mechanicsville.

STATISTICS OF COTTON MANUFACTORIES

IN FALL RIVER.

	In-cor-p'd.	Bls. Cotton used per ann.	Yards of Cloth manufactured per annum.	No. Hands Empl'd.	M'nth'ly Pay Roll.
1	1852	9,000	22,000,000	1,100	$22,000
2	1825	1,200	2,250,000	140	3,000
3	1874	3,750	9,250,000	350	8.500
4	1872	9,250	24,000,000	900	22,500
5	1871	5,000	12,500,000	425	12,000
6	1871	3,500	6,000,000	340	9,000
7	1867	3,500	5,500,000	375	11,000
8	1866	10,500	23,000,000	950	22,500
9	1813	3,000	7,000,000	330	7,000
10	1875	800	9,000,000	120	3,500
11	1848	1,500	3,500,000	175	4,500
12	1872	5,000	13,000,000	500	12,000
13	1863	9,000	23,000,000	800	22,500
14	1871	3,000	5,500,000	425	12,000
15	1868	6,250	15,000,000	550	16,000
16	1867	10,000	25,000,000	850	24,000
17	1847	2,750	6,750,000	325	7,500
18	1871	3,000	2,250,000	150	3,750
19	1867	675	1,225,000	135	3,500
20	1871	3,500	9,000,000	325	8,500
21	1871	4,500	11,500,000	350	12,000
22	1822	3,000	7,000,000	475	10,500
23	1871	5,000	12,500,000	450	11,500
24	1867	2,750	9,000,000	275	7,000
25	1872	4,500	12,000,000	450	12,500
26	1872	4,500	12,000,000	425	11,000
27	1871	4,250	11,000,000	350	10,000
28	1871	4,000	10,000,000	350	9,500
29	1866	5,000	12,500,000	425	13,000
30	1814	4,000	10,250,000	375	10,500
31	1859	5,000	12,500,000	500	13,500
32	1871	3,250	8,250,000	325	7,500
33	1871	4,000	10,000,000	360	9,250
		147,925	363,225,000	14,375	$372,500

PAY-DAY OF THE SEVERAL CORPORATIONS

IN FALL RIVER.

American Linen Co.,	Third Thursday,
American Print Works,	Second Thursday,
Anawan Manufactory,	Second Wednesday,
Barnard Manufacturing Co.,	Second "
Border City Mills,	Fourth "
Chace Mills,	Second "
Crescent Mills,	Second "
Davol Mills,	First "
Durfee Mills,	Second "
Fall River Bleachery,	Fourth "
Fall River Iron Works Co.,	Second "
Fall River Manufactory,	First "
Fall River Merino Company,	15th of Month,
Fall River Print Works,	10th "
Flint Mills,	1st or 2d Wednesday,
Granite Mills,	Second "
King Philip Mills.	Fourth "
Mechanics' Mills,	Third "
Merchants' Manufg. Co.,	Second "
Metacomet Mills,	Second "
Montaup Mills,	Second "
Mount Hope Mills,	Second "
Narragansett Mills,	First "
Osborn Mills,	First "
Pocasset Manufg. Co.,	Second Thursday,
Richard Borden Manufg. Co.	Third Wednesday,
Robeson Mills,	Second Tuesday,
Sagamore Mills,	Second Wednesday,
Shove Mills,	Second "
Slade Mills,	Second "
Stafford Mills,	Second "
Tecumseh Mills,	1st or 2d "
Troy C. & W. Manufactory,	Second "
Union Mill Company,	First "
Wamsutta St'm Woolen Mill,	Fourth Friday,
Wampanoag Mills,	1st or 2d Wednesday,
Weetamoe Mills,	Second "

Organization of Corporations,

January, 1878.

American Linen Co.

PRESIDENT: Jefferson Borden.
CLERK AND TREASURER: Walter Paine, 3d.
DIRECTORS: Jefferson Borden, Philip D. Borden, Richard B. Borden, George B. Durfee, Walter Paine, 3d.
Annual Meeting—2d Wednesday in February.

American Print Works.

PRESIDENT: Jefferson Borden.
CLERK: George B. Durfee.
AGENT AND TREASURER: Thos. J. Borden.
DIRECTORS: Thos. J. Borden, Jefferson Borden, Holder B. Durfee, Geo. B. Durfee, W. B. Durfee.
Annual Meeting—1st Tuesday in August.

Annawan Manufactory.

PRESIDENT: Jefferson Borden.
CLERK: Richard B. Borden.
TREASURER: Thomas S. Borden.
DIRECTORS: Jefferson Borden, Wm. B. Durfee, R. B. Borden, Holder B. Durfee, Thos. S. Borden.
Annual Meeting—1st Tuesday in August.

Barnard Manufacturing Co.

PRESIDENT: Louis L. Barnard.
CLERK AND TREASURER: Nathaniel B. Borden.
DIRECTORS: L. L. Barnard, Stephen Davol,
Wm. H. Jennings, Arnold B. Chace, Robert T.
Davis, Simeon Borden, James M. Aldrich, N. B.
Borden, Alphonso S. Covel, John Campbell, W.
H. Gifford.
Annual Meeting—3d Thursday in October.

Border City Mills.

PRESIDENT: James A. Hathaway.
CLERK AND TREASURER: Geo. T. Hathaway.
DIRECTORS: James A. Hathaway, S. A. Chace,
Job T. Wilson, Stephen Davol, Chas. P. Stick-
ney, Elijah C. Kilburn, Chester W. Greene, Geo.
T. Hathaway, Holder B. Durfee, Isaac Smith,
George Parsons.
Annual Meeting—4th Wednesday in October.

Chace Mills.

PRESIDENT: Augustus Chace.
CLERK AND TREASURER: Joseph A. Baker.
DIRECTORS: Augustus Chace, Cook Borden,
James Henry, George W. Grinnell, Robert K.
Remington, Edward E. Hathaway, Wm. Mason,
Chas. P. Stickney, Joseph A. Baker.
Annual Meeting—In October.

Crescent Mills.

PRESIDENT: Benjamin Covel.
CLERK AND TREASURER: Alphonso S. Covel.
DIRECTORS: Benjamin Covel, Daniel A. Chapin,
Wm. B. Durfee, Alphonso S. Covel, Griffits M.
Haffards, David F. Brown, John F. Nichols,
Lafayette Nichols, Wm. H. Ashley.
Annual Meeting—2d Wednesday in February.

Davol Mills.

PRESIDENT: William C. Davol.
CLERK AND TREASURER: Wm. C. Davol, Jr.
DIRECTORS: Wm. C. Davol, Charles P. Stickney, Foster H. Stafford, Frank S. Stevens, Jonathan Slade, John P. Slade, Wm. W. Stewart, Edward E. Hathaway, W. C. Davol, Jr.
Annual Meeting—In April.

Durfee Mills.

PRESIDENT: John S. Brayton.
CLERK: David A. Brayton, Jr.
TREASURER: David A. Brayton.
DIRECTORS: John S. Brayton, David A. Brayton, Israel P. Brayton.
Annual Meeting—In October.

Fall River Bleachery.

PRESIDENT: Jefferson Borden.
CLERK AND TREASURER: Spencer Borden.
DIRECTORS: Jefferson Borden, Spencer Borden, Richard B. Borden, Philip D. Borden, Bradford D. Davol, Thos. Bennett, Jr., George B. Durfee, Crawford E. Lindsey, Edward D. Mandell.
Annual Meeting—3d Thursday in May.

Fall River Iron Works Co.

PRESIDENT: Jefferson Borden.
CLERK AND TREASURER: Robert C. Brown.
DIRECTORS: Jefferson Borden, John S. Brayton, Wm. B. Durfee, Richard B. Borden, Holder B. Durfee.
Annual Meeting—1st Tuesday in August.

Fall River Manufactory.

PRESIDENT: Holder B. Durfee.
CLERK: John S. Brayton.
TREASURER: S. Angier Chace.
DIRECTORS: Holder B. Durfee, John S. Brayton, S. Angier Chace, James M. Anthony, Christopher Borden.
Annual Meeting—2d Tuesday in March.

Fall River Manufacturers' Mutual Ins. Co.

PRESIDENT: Stephen Davol,
SECRETARY AND TREASURER: Isaac B. Chace.
DIRECTORS: Stephen Davol, S. A. Chace, D. A. Brayton, T. J. Borden, Jefferson Borden, Wm. H. Jennings, Walter Paine, 3d, I. B. Chace, P. D. Borden, R. B. Borden. E. C. Kilburn, Andrew G. Pierce, Geo. T. Hathaway, T. F. Eddy, George B. Durfee.
Annual Meeting—1st Wednesday in March.

Fall River Merino Co.

PRESIDENT: Frank S. Stevens.
CLERK AND TREASURER: Seth H. Wetherbee.
DIRECTORS: Frank S. Stevens, Foster H. Stafford, Robert T. Davis, Wm. Mason, Samuel M. Luther, Danforth Horton, John D. Flint, Samuel Wadington, Samuel W. Flint, S. H. Wetherbee.
Annual Meeting—4th Thursday in January.

Fall River Print Works.

PRESIDENT: Linden Cook.
CLERK AND TREASURER: Andrew Robeson.
DIRECTORS: Linden Cook, Charles P. Stickney, Andrew Robeson.
Annual Meeting—4th Wednesday in January.

Fall River Railroad.

PRESIDENT: Harrison Bliss.
CLERK AND TREASURER: E. D. Hewins.
DIRECTORS: Harrison Bliss, Worcester; N.
Thayer, Jr., Lancaster; William J. Rotch, J. A.
Beauvais, New Bedford; John H. Perry, Boston;
Wm. Rotch, Fall River; Chas. T. Bonney, New
Bedford; Wm. H. Bliss, Worcester; E. D. Hewins, Fitchburg.
Annual Meeting—2d Thursday in December.

Fall River Spool and Bobbin Co.

PRESIDENT: Cook Borden.
CLERK: Bradford D. Davol.
TREASURER: J. Henry Wells.
DIRECTORS: Cook Borden, F. H. Stafford, Wm.
H. Jennings, Stephen Davol, Joseph Healy, S A.
Chace, Aug. Chace, Frank L. Almy, B. D. Davol.
Annual Meeting—Last Tuesday in October.

Flint Mills.

PRESIDENT: John D. Flint.
CLERK AND TREASURER: George H. Eddy.
DIRECTORS: John D. Flint, Wm. H. Jennings,
Simeon Borden, Frank L. Almy, Gardner T.
Dean, George H. Eddy, Junius P. Prentiss,
Samuel W. Flint, B. D. Davol.
Annual Meeting—1st Monday in November.

Granite Mills.

PRESIDENT: William Mason.
CLERK AND TREASURER: Charles M. Shove.
DIRECTORS: W. Mason, Edmund Chase, Chas.
P. Stickney, John S. Brayton, Iram Smith, John
P. Slade, Charles M. Shove.
Annual Meeting—4th Monday in October.

King Philip Mills.

PRESIDENT: Crawford E. Lindsey.
CLERK: Azariah S. Tripp.
TREASURER: Elijah C. Kilburn.
DIRECTORS: C. E. Lindsey, James Henry, S.
Angier Chace, Philip D. Borden, E. C. Kilburn,
Simeon Borden, Charles H. Dean, Wm. Lindsey,
Edwin Shaw, Charles P. Dring, Daniel Stillwell.
Annual Meeting—Last Thursday in October.

Manufacturers' Board of Trade.

PRESIDENT: Walter Paine, 3d.
VICE-PRESIDENT: George T. Hathaway.
SECRETARY: Simeon B. Chase.
TREASURER: Isaac B. Chace.
Annual Meeting—3d Friday in January.

Manufacturers' Gas Co.

PRESIDENT: S. Angier Chace.
CLERK AND TREASURER: Chas. P. Stickney.
DIRECTORS: S. Angier Chace, Augustus Chace,
Chas. P. Stickney, David A. Brayton, William C.
Davol, Jr., Foster H. Stafford, Thomas F. Eddy,
Joseph A. Baker.
Annual Meeting—In June.

Mechanics Mills.

PRESIDENT: Stephen Davol.
CLERK: James M. Morton, Jr.
TREASURER: George B. Durfee.
DIRECTORS: Stephen Davol, Job B. French,
Thomos J. Borden, George B. Durfee, Tillinghast
Records, Southard H. Miller, James M. Morton,
Jr., John B. Hathaway, F. S. Stevens.
Annual Meeting—1st Thursday in February.

Merchants Manufacturing Co.

PRESIDENT: James Henry.
CLERK AND TREASURER: Wm H. Jennings.
DIRECTORS: James Henry, William H. Jennings, Augustus Chace, Robert S. Gibbs, Charles H. Dean, Crawford E. Lindsey, James M. Osborn, Richard B. Borden, Robert T. Davis.
Annual Meeting—4th Wednesday in January.

Metacomet Mill.

AGENT: Thomas S. Borden.
Owned by the Fall River Iron Works Co.

Montaup Mills.

PRESIDENT: George B. Durfee.
CLERK AND TREASURER: Isaac Borden.
DIRECTORS: George B. Durfee, Isaac Borden, Thomas J. Borden, William L. Slade, Holder B. Durfee, William Valentine, Bradford D. Davol, Weaver Osborn, Wm. H. Ashley, Benj. Hall.
Annual Meeting—4th Monday in October.

Mount Hope Mill.

AGENT: Jefferson Borden, Jr.
Owned by American Print Works.

Narragansett Mills.

PRESIDENT: Holder B. Durfee.
CLERK AND TREASURER: James Waring.
DIRECTORS: Holder B. Durfee, James Waring, Foster H. Stafford, David T. Wilcox, James P. Hillard, Robert Henry, Samuel Wadington, Wm. Beattie, George W. Nowell.
Annual Meeting—In October

Old Colony Railroad Co.

PRESIDENT: Charles F. Choate.
CLERK: George Marston.
TREASURER: John M. Washburn.
DIRECTORS: Onslow Stearns, Uriel Crocker, Charles F. Choate, F. B. Hayes, Boston; Fred. L. Ames, Easton; Samuel L. Crocker, Taunton: Jacob H. Loud, Plymouth; J. S. Brayton, T. J. Borden, Fall River; R. W. Turner, Randolph; E. N. Winslow, Hyannis; George Marston, New Bedford; Elisha W. Willard, Newport.
Annual Meeting—4th Tuesday in November.

Old Colony Steamboat Co.

PRESIDENT: Onslow Stearns.
CLERK: Charles F. Choate.
TREASURER: John M Washburn.
DIRECTORS: Onslow Stearns: C. F. Choate, Silas Pierce, Jr., Boston; Benj. Finch, Newport; T. J. Borden, C. P. Stickney, Fall River; Fred. L. Ames, Easton; Wm. Borden, Cornelius Bliss, New York.
Annual Meeting—4th Tuesday in June.

Osborn Mills.

PRESIDENT: Weaver Osborn.
CLERK AND TREASURER: Joseph Healy.
DIRECTORS: Weaver Osborn, Frank S. Stevens, Charles P. Stickney, Joseph Osborn, John C. Milne, Joseph Healy, Edward E. Hathaway, Geo. T. Hathaway, Benjamin Hall, George W. Gibbs, Charles H. Dean.
Annual Meeting—Last Tuesday in April.

Pocasset Manufacturing Co.

PRESIDENT: Samuel W. Rodman.
CLERK AND TREASURER: Bradford D. Davol.
AGENT: Henry S. Howe.
DIRECTORS: Samuel W. Rodman, Stephen Davol, Horatio Hathaway, Edward Motley, F. M. Weld, Jr.
Annual Meeting—Last Monday in February.

Richard Borden Manufacturing Co.

PRESIDENT: Thomas J. Borden.
CLERK AND TREASURER: Richard B. Borden.
DIRECTORS: Rich'd B. Borden, Thos. J. Borden, Philip D. Borden, A. S. Covel, Edw'd P. Borden.
Annual Meeting—2d Tuesday in November.

Robeson Mills.

PRESIDENT: Charles P. Stickney.
CLERK AND TREASURER: Louis Robeson.
DIRECTORS: Charles P. Stickney, Wm. R. Robeson, Linden Cook, Wm. C. Davol, Jr., Frank S. Stevens, Louis Robeson, E. E. Hathaway.
Annual Meeting—1st Monday in February.

Sagamore Mills.

PRESIDENT: James A. Hathaway.
CLERK AND TREASURER: Geo. T. Hathaway.
DIRECTORS: James A. Hathaway, Job T. Wilson, Josiah C. Blaisdell, John D. Flint, Chas. P. Stickney, George T. Hathaway, Jas. E. Cunneen, John M. Deane, Chester W. Greene.
Annual Meeting—4th Monday in October.

Shove Mills.

PRESIDENT: John P. Slade.
CLERK AND TREASURER: George A. Chace.
DIRECTORS: John P. Slade, George A. Chace,
William Mason, of Taunton; Edmund Chace,
Lloyd S. Earle, Josiah C. Blaisdell, Isaac W.
Howland, Charles M. Shove, H. B. Allen,
Asa Pettey, Joseph E. Macomber, Clark Shove,
George W. Slade.
Annual Meeting—In February.

Slade Mills.

PRESIDENT: William L. Slad .
CLERK AND TREASURER: Henry S. Fenner.
DIRECTORS: Wm. L. Slade, S. Angier Chace,
Jerome Dwelly, W. Valentine, Frank S. Stevens,
Richard B. Borden, Benjamin Hall, James M.
Osborn, Jonathan Slade, John C. Milne, Daniel
Wilbur.
Annual Meeting—Last Tuesday in January.

Stafford Mills.

PRESIDENT: Foster H. Stafford.
CLERK AND TREASURER—Shubael P. Lovell.
AGENT: Foster H. Stafford.
DIRECTORS: F. H. Stafford, Wm. C. Davol,
Charles P. Stickney, Robert T. Davis, Edmund
Chase, Danforth Horton, Wm. L, Slade, Weaver
Osborn, William Mason.
Annual Meeting—4th Tuesday in January.

Tecumseh Mills.

PRESIDENT: Augustus Chace.
CLERK AND TREASURER: Simeon B. Chase.
DIRECTORS: Augustus Chace, Cook Borden,
Jona. T. Lincoln, Andrew M. Jenning, Samuel
Wadington, D. T. Wilcox, John Southworth, S.
B. Chase, George E. Hoar.
Annual Meeting—4th Tuesday in October.

Troy Cotton and Woolen Manufactory.

PRESIDENT: Jefferson Borden.
CLERK AND TREASURER: Richard B. Borden.
DIRECTORS: Jefferson Borden, Stephen Davol,
Thomas J. Borden, John S. Brayton, Richard B.
Borden.
Annual Meeting—1st Tuesday in February.

Union Belt Company.

PRESIDENT: Richard B. Borden.
CLERK AND TREASURER: A. S. Covel.
AGENT: William H. Chace.
DIRECTORS: R. B. Borden, Walter Paine, 3d,
B. D. Davol, Wm. H. Chace, A. S. Covel, E. C.
Kilburn, T. J. Borden.
Annual Meeting—3d Thursday in January.

Union Mill Company.

PRESIDENT: Charles P. Dring.
CLERK AND TREASURER: S. Angier Chace.
DIRECTORS: Charles P. Dring, S. Angier Chace,
Wm. Mason, Elijah C. Kilburn, Foster H. Staf-
ford, Holder B. Durfee, Southard H. Miller, David
T. Wilcox, Simeon B. Chase, George H. Hills.
Annual Meeting—3d Monday in January.

Wampanoag Mills.

PRESIDENT: Robert T. Davis.
CLERK AND TREASURER—Walter C. Durfee.
DIRECTORS: Robert T. Davis, W. C. Durfee, John D. Flint, Stephen Davol, Foster H. Stafford, Wm. H. Jennings, George H. Eddy, Lloyd S. Earle, Simeon Borden, Alphonso S. Covel, John H. Boone.
Annual Meeting—4th Monday in January.

Weetamoe Mills.

PRESIDENT: Job B. French.
CLERK: John E. Blaisdell.
TREASURER: William Lindsey.
DIRECTORS: Job B. French, Elijah C. Kilburn, Josiah C. Blaisdell, Francis B. Hood, Henry C. Lincoln, Wm. Lindsey, John P. Slade, William H. Ashley, Charles H Dean.
Annual Meeting—4th Wednesday in January.

F. R., Warren & Prov. R. R. Co.

PRESIDENT: Onslow Stearns.
CLERK: John S Brayton.
TREASURER: John M. Washburn.
DIRECTORS: Onslow Stearns, Chas. F. Choate, Boston; J. S. Brayton, T. J. Borden, Fall River; Benj. Finch, Newport; E. N. Winslow, Hyannis.
Annual Meeting—2d Monday in March.

www.ingramcontent.com/pod-product-compliance
Lightning Source LLC
Chambersburg PA
CBHW031820090426
42739CB00008B/1347